In Other Words

In Other Words

John Mortimer

VIKING
an imprint of
PENGUIN BOOKS

VIKING

Published by the Penguin Group
Penguin Books Ltd, 80 Strand, London WC2R ORL, England
Penguin Group (USA) Inc., 375 Hudson Street, New York, New York 10014, USA
Penguin Group (Canada), 90 Eglinton Avenue East, Suite 700, Toronto, Ontario, Canada M4P 2Y3
(a division of Pearson Penguin Canada Inc.)
Penguin Ireland, 25 St Stephen's Green, Dublin 2, Ireland (a division of Penguin Books Ltd)
Penguin Group (Australia), 250 Camberwell Road,
Camberwell, Victoria 3124, Australia (a division of Pearson Australia Group Pty Ltd)
Penguin Books India Pvt Ltd, 11 Community Centre,
Panchsheel Park, New Delhi – 110 017, India
Penguin Group (NZ), 67 Apollo Drive, Rosedale, North Shore 0632, New Zealand
(a division of Pearson New Zealand Ltd)
Penguin Books (South Africa) (Pty) Ltd, 24 Sturdee Avenue,
Rosebank, Johannesburg 2196, South Africa

Penguin Books Ltd, Registered Offices: 80 Strand, London WC2R ORL, England

www.penguin.com

First published in 2008
1

Printed in Great Britain by Clays Ltd, St Ives plc

A CIP catalogue record for this book is available from the British Library

ISBN: 978-0-670-91787-7

www.greenpenguin.co.uk

To all the performers, actors and musicians
who have joined in bringing
these other words to life

Introduction

I was fortunate enough to grow up in a home where quotations from poetry were part of the daily conversation. My father, a blind barrister, apparently knew most of the plays of Shakespeare by heart. He would take me every year to see the plays in the repertoire at what was then called the Shakespeare Memorial Theatre. We weren't the most popular members of the audience because my father liked a six-course dinner, but when we arrived at our seats, usually about ten minutes late, in the front row of the stalls, he was of enormous assistance to the actors, being able to say the lines about five seconds before they could get to them.

At home, from my earliest years, I was never quite sure whether it was my father or Shakespeare who was speaking. One of his most frequent questions to me was, 'Is execution done on Cawdor?' At the age of six, I found this difficult to answer. Among my earliest memories was reading the scene between Orsino and Viola in *Twelfth Night*. Viola tells of a love-stricken woman who 'sat like patience on a monument'. I can't count the number of times I heard my father tell various courts that during the no doubt misguided opposition's speeches he had managed to 'sit like patience on a monument'.

Shakespeare slipped as easily in and out of our conversation as though he had been invented especially for us. It wasn't until I went away to school that I discovered contemporary poetry and, in particular, Auden. Daydreaming in class, I saw myself fighting in the Spanish Civil War, drinking sangria as I reloaded my automatic rifle, muttering, 'The desires of the heart are as crooked as corkscrews.'

Moving on to the loneliness of a public school, I discovered a friend and a writer whom I have enjoyed all my life. Unfortunately, Byron was no longer at Harrow, but his slippers and curled dagger were still in the library and I could lie by the tomb in the churchyard where he lay to write poetry. It now commands a clear view of Ruislip and the gasworks. There are few writers who can move as easily from a perfectly romantic lyric such as 'So, we'll go no more a-roving' to a ruthlessly detached and horrifying description of an Italian execution. *Don Juan* is a comic masterpiece and I think one of the most endearing things about Byron was his constant ability to laugh at himself.

For a long time I had thought of poetry as a solitary pleasure, to be read in lonely moments, to be learned by heart and repeated with internal joy on the tops of buses or waiting in doctors' surgeries.

The poets I knew – Dylan Thomas, Sidney Keyes, Michael Hamburger and Laurie Lee – all seemed to find the work almost superhumanly difficult, and they would put off the moment of composition by doing almost anything else, in Laurie Lee's case reading carefully through all the shipping news in *The Times* extremely slowly. However, it was a time for poetry and the Soho pubs were haunted by poets either stuck for a line or triumphantly shouting an achieved verse. I spent evenings with Dylan Thomas as he recited his verses, retiring at intervals to make use of the women's lavatory, which he claimed he was entitled to use as a 'creature of indeterminate sex'. When we were particularly brave, these voyages would end up in the offices of *Horizon*, a magazine edited by Cyril Connolly which actually published poetry. The few poems that I wrote then were greatly influenced by Auden and have not, I am pleased to say, survived.

I had begun writing for the theatre and it occurred to me that the poetry of my friends and others could be taken out of the lonely rooms and allowed to appear in public.

I got together a group of actors and we started to plan a programme of these much loved and silently treasured pieces of poetry and prose. The words would be taken off the page and show their strengths in a public performance. In time we added music and Jon Lord, formerly of Deep Purple and now a classical composer, wrote a score to accompany some of the poems.

With a succession of expert performers the show *Mortimer's Miscellany* has been on tours in a number of countries, which have included America, Australia and Belgium.

So here it is as a book. I hope that everyone will find some poems to love and remember in it. If you do, try reading them aloud, either at crowded parties or on lonely beaches, and let the words fight for themselves.

Act One

'As I walked out one evening'

As I walked out one evening,
  Walking down Bristol Street,
The crowds upon the pavement
  Were fields of harvest wheat.

And down by the brimming river
  I heard a lover sing
Under an arch of the railway:
  'Love has no ending.

'I'll love you, dear, I'll love you
  Till China and Africa meet,
And the river jumps over the mountain
  And the salmon sing in the street,

'I'll love you till the ocean
  Is folded and hung up to dry
And the seven stars go squawking
  Like geese about the sky.

'The years shall run like rabbits,
  For in my arms I hold

The Flower of the Ages,
  And the first love of the world.'

But all the clocks in the city
  Began to whirr and chime:
  'O let not Time deceive you,
  You cannot conquer Time.

'In the burrows of the Nightmare
  Where Justice naked is,
Time watches from the shadow
  And coughs when you would kiss.

'In headaches and in worry
  Vaguely life leaks away,
And Time will have his fancy
  To-morrow or to-day.

'Into many a green valley
  Drifts the appalling snow;
Time breaks the threaded dances
  And the diver's brilliant bow.

'O plunge your hands in water,
  Plunge them in up to the wrist;

Stare, stare in the basin
    And wonder what you've missed.

'The glacier knocks in the cupboard,
    The desert sighs in the bed,
And the crack in the tea-cup opens
    A lane to the land of the dead.

'Where the beggars raffle the banknotes
    And the Giant is enchanting to Jack,
And the Lily-white Boy is a Roarer,
    And Jill goes down on her back.

'O look, look in the mirror,
    O look in your distress;
Life remains a blessing
    Although you cannot bless.

'O stand, stand at the window
    As the tears scald and start;
You shall love your crooked neighbour
    With your crooked heart.'

It was late, late in the evening,
    The lovers they were gone;

The clocks had ceased their chiming
And the deep river ran on.

That was written by W. H. Auden during the dark days when Europe was cracking in to war, dark days for Europe and dark days for me.

I remember Winston Churchill coming to Harrow when I was a schoolboy and joining in the songs. He seemed about 110 and I said to my friend, 'If they ever put him in charge of the war, we've had it!'

Of course I was wrong.

I was the only child of a blind barrister father who bore his affliction with considerable courage and humour. His blindness didn't, I think, make him feel useless, as Milton did in his great poem of discontent.

On His Blindness

When I consider how my light is spent,
   E're half my days, in this dark world and wide,
   And that one Talent which is death to hide,
   Lodg'd with me useless, though my Soul more bent
To serve therewith my Maker, and present
   My true account, least he returning chide,
   'Doth God exact day-labour, light deny'd,'
   I fondly ask; But patience to prevent
That murmur, soon replies, God doth not need
   Either man's work or his own gifts, who best
   Bear his milde yoak, they serve him best, his State
Is Kingly. Thousands at his bidding speed
   And post o'er Land and Ocean without rest:
They also serve who only stand and waite.

My father's retinas left the backs of his eyes when I was about sixteen years old. He could clearly remember us and didn't have to have my mother miraculously brought to him out of the darkness as Milton wrote in his second poem on his blindness.

On His Deceased Wife

Methought I saw my late espousèd Saint
  Brought to me like Alcestis from the grave,
  Whom Jove's great Son to her glad Husband
    gave,
  Rescu'd from death by force though pale and
    faint,
Mine as whom washt from spot of child-bed taint,
  Purification in the old Law did save,
  And such, as yet once more I trust to have
  Full sight of her in Heaven without restraint,
Came vested all in white, pure as her mind:
  Her face was vail'd, yet to my fancied sight,
  Love, sweetness, goodness, in her person shin'd

So clear, as in no face with more delight.
But O as to embrace me she enclin'd,
I wak'd, she fled, and day brought back mý night.

My father's divorce practice grew rather than diminished in the war years and I was fed, clothed and educated almost entirely on the proceeds of cruelty, adultery and wilful refusal to provide regular intercourse. My father used to come home with tales of his triumphs in court, such as having been able to prove adultery by the evidence of footprints upside-down on the dashboard of an Austin Seven motor car parked in Hampstead Garden Suburb. So, early in my life, it was decided that I should become a lawyer.

'It is sure that honesty, learning, reliability and common sense *might* all be united in the person of a lawyer. It is also sure that they never were.'

That was John Wilkes on lawyers. I have largely steered clear of legal anecdotes in this selection. They always seem to me rather cruel and, although hilarious to judges and lawyers, those sentenced to death or long terms of imprisonment rarely join in the laughter.

For example:

JUDGE TO CONVICTED MURDERER: Have
   you anything to say why sentence of death
   should not be passed upon you?
MURDERER: Bugger all, My Lord.
JUDGE TO COUNSEL: Mr Bleaks, did your client
   say something?
MR BLEAKS: Bugger all, My Lord.
JUDGE: Funny, I could swear I heard him say
   something . . .

These extracts bring back memories of various judges
at the Old Bailey. There was one delightful judge
who used to adjourn the court halfway through
the morning for a glass of chilled Chablis and a
little nibble of Stilton cheese. He had to sentence a
totally drunk Irish labourer who was swaying, still
drunk, pink-eyed, in the dock after having been
rightly arrested for peeing down the stairs of Leicester
Square tube station, indecent assault and insulting a
police officer. And the judge told him that he was
prepared to put him on probation provided he never
touched another drop of alcohol for the remainder
of his life.

'Nothing, Your Holiness, not a drop shall pass my lips.'

'But by nothing, I mean absolutely nothing,' the judge was more specific. 'Not even the *teeniest, weeniest*, little dry sherry before your dinner.'

It was the same judge who had the unhappy duty of sentencing two men who had been found in an attitude of unusual friendliness under Waterloo Bridge.

'You two men have been found guilty of a terrible act,' the judge said, 'which has been cursed down history. The mere mention of which can make strong women faint and men vomit. And what makes it so much worse is that you chose to do it under one of the most *beautiful* bridges in London.'

It has also been suggested that he added, 'You two men should go away and pull yourselves together.'

It was around this time that a noble lord, Lord Arran, introduced into the House of Lords a bill which permitted men of a certain age to be as friendly as they liked. Lord Arran was happily married, with a wife who embroidered his shirts above his heart with his coronet and his initials. For this reason he was always known to his many friends as the Greater Crested Tit.

Apart from the Sexual Offences Bill, Lord Arran passed a statute for the preservation of wildlife, and in particular for the preservation of badgers. As he lay dying, he asked a friend at his bedside why it was that the House of Lords had been packed full, with peers almost falling out of the public gallery, 'when I passed my buggers bill, but almost completely empty except for a few old earls when I passed my badgers bill'. It took his friend to remind him that 'there are very few badgers in the House of Lords'.

Many poets have been imprisoned, but few have written about it as memorably as Oscar Wilde in his great poem *The Ballad of Reading Gaol*. Here's the first section:

The Ballad of Reading Gaol

He did not wear his scarlet coat,
    For blood and wine are red,
And blood and wine were on his hands
    When they found him with the dead,
The poor dead woman whom he loved,
    And murdered in her bed.

He walked amongst the Trial Men
    In a suit of shabby grey;
A cricket cap was on his head,
    And his step seemed light and gay;
But I never saw a man who looked
    So wistfully at the day.

I never saw a man who looked
   With such a wistful eye
Upon that little tent of blue
   Which prisoners call the sky,
And at every drifting cloud that went
   With sails of silver by.

I walked, with other souls in pain,
   Within another ring,
And was wondering if the man had done
   A great or little thing,
When a voice behind me whispered low,
   'That fellow's got to swing.'

Dear Christ! the very prison walls
   Suddenly seemed to reel,
And the sky above my head became
   Like a casque of scorching steel;
And, though I was a soul in pain,
   My pain I could not feel.

I only knew what hunted thought
   Quickened his step, and why
He looked upon the garish day
   With such a wistful eye;

The man had killed the thing he loved,
　　And so he had to die.

Yet each man kills the thing he loves
　　By each let this be heard,
Some do it with a bitter look,
　　Some with a flattering word,
The coward does it with a kiss,
　　The brave man with a sword!

Some kill their love when they are young,
　　And some when they are old;
Some strangle with the hands of Lust,
　　Some with the hands of Gold:
The kindest use a knife, because
　　The dead so soon grow cold.

Some love too little, some too long,
　　Some sell, and others buy;
Some do the deed with many tears,
　　And some without a sigh:
For each man kills the thing he loves,
　　Yet each man does not die.

He does not die a death of shame
   On a day of dark disgrace,
Nor have a noose about his neck,
   Nor a cloth upon his face,
Nor drop feet foremost through the floor
   Into an empty space.

He does not sit with silent men
   Who watch him night and day;
Who watch him when he tries to weep,
   And when he tries to pray;
Who watch him lest himself should rob
   The prison of its prey.

He does not wake at dawn to see
   Dread figures throng his room,
The shivering Chaplain robed in white,
   The Sheriff stern with gloom,
And the Governor all in shiny black,
   With the yellow face of Doom.

He does not rise in piteous haste
   To put on convict-clothes,
While some coarse-mouthed Doctor gloats,
   and notes

Each new and nerve-twitched pose,
Fingering a watch whose little ticks
Are like horrible hammer-blows.

He does not know that sickening thirst
That sands one's throat, before
The hangman with his gardener's gloves
Slips through the padded door,
And binds one with three leathern thongs,
That the throat may thirst no more.

He does not bend his head to hear
The Burial Office read,
Nor, while the terror of his soul
Tells him he is not dead,
Cross his own coffin, as he moves
Into the hideous shed.

He does not stare upon the air
Through a little roof of glass;
He does not pray with lips of clay
For his agony to pass;
Nor feel upon his shuddering cheek
The kiss of Caiaphas.

When I said goodbye to my clients on their way to prison, I think they had no idea what it would be like if it was their first sentence. There's a terrible sameness about prisons. There's a familiar prison smell built up by years of chamber pots being slopped in and slopped out. There is a feeling of lives wasted, of everybody doing not very much. Probably the worst punishment that prison inflicts is that of boredom, and its great lesson is to make sure that your life is as interesting as possible before you feel the touch of a finger on your collar.

I decided I needed a character like Sherlock Holmes or Maigret to provide for me in my old age, and I thought of Rumpole. He spends a hard life convincing unsympathetic courts of the virtues of Magna Carta and the Petition of Right.

He hasn't been an unmixed blessing and can cause me some embarrassment. You can't go into El Vino's in Fleet Street (the original Pommeroy's Wine Bar) without finding at least eight middle-aged barristers drinking indifferent claret and claiming to be the original Rumpole. After one disastrous appearance in court my client said to me, 'Your Mr Rumpole could have won this case for me. I don't know why you couldn't.'

My legal career came to an end in Singapore. I had gone there to defend a solicitor MP who was alleged to have stolen money from the gift shop in the Hilton.

I entered the robing room, where we put on our wigs and gowns, in the Central Criminal Court in Singapore. The Chinese lady who was brewing Nescafé and handing out cough mixture for barristers with sore throats greeted me with, 'Ho, there you are! Lumpole of the Bay-ree.'

The Chinese and Indians are, on the whole, unfriendly to each other. We had a Chinese judge and an Indian prosecutor, to whom I was mildly rude in the course of an argument. The prosecutor then asked the judge if he might have time off to recover from my attack. The judge refused to allow this and so the case wound wearily on. In the course of the case, we discovered that the only missing things from the gift shop were packets of sweets and views of the harbour and such like trivialities. I had done exciting cases previously in Singapore and in one I had the pleasure of cross-examining the President in a libel action he had brought against an opposition MP. That was a case worth remembering, but the same could not be said for the matter of the Singapore Hilton.

I knew then that I couldn't spend my declining years travelling round the Far East and being hailed as 'Lumpole of the Bay-ree'. And so I decided to give up practising law and stick to writing.

I thought this collection should include a Rumpole scene, but what follows has got nothing to do with law courts or the law. It's Rumpole in a smart restaurant.

Now, my wife, Hilda, is a good plain cook. In saying that, I'm not referring to She Who Must Be Obeyed's moral values or passing any judgement on her personal appearance. What I can tell you is that she cooks without flights of fancy.

She is not, in any way, a woman who lacks imagination. Indeed, some of the things she imagines Rumpole gets up to when out of her sight are colourful in the extreme, but she doesn't apply such gifts to a chop or a potato, being quite content to grill one and boil the other. She can also boil a cabbage into submission and fry fish. The nearest her cooking comes to the poetic is, perhaps, in her baked jam roll, which I have always found to be an emotion best recollected in tranquillity.

From all this you will gather that Hilda's honest cooking is sufficient but not exotic, and that happily the terrible curse of 'nouvelle cuisine' has not yet infected Froxbury Mansions in the Gloucester Road.

So it is not often I am confronted with the sort of fare photographed in the Sunday supplements. I scarcely ever sit down to an octagonal plate on which a sliver of monkfish is arranged in a composition of pastel shades, which also features a brush stroke of pink sauce, a single peeled prawn and a sprig of dill. Such gluttony is, happily, beyond my means.

It wasn't, however, beyond the means of Hilda's cousin Everard, who was visiting us from Canada, where he carries on a thriving trade as a company lawyer. He told us that he felt we stood in dire need of what he called 'a taste of gracious living' and booked a table for three at La Maison Jean-Pierre.

WAITER: *Madame, messieurs.* Tonight Jean-Pierre recommends, for the main course, *la poésie de la poitrine du canard aux céleri et épinard cru.*

HILDA: *Poésie* . . . That's poetry, Rumpole. Tastes a good deal better than that old Wordsworth of yours, I shouldn't be surprised.

RUMPOLE: Tell us about it, Georges. Whet our appetite.

WAITER: A wafer-thin slice of breast of duck, marinated in a drop or two of Armagnac, delicately grilled and served with a celery remoulade and some leaves of spinach lightly steamed.

RUMPOLE: And mash . . . ?

WAITER: (Unable to believe his ears) *Excusez-moi?*

RUMPOLE: Mashed spuds come with it, do they?

HILDA: Ssh, Rumpole! (Charmingly to Georges) I will have the *poésie*. It sounds delicious.

RUMPOLE: I would like a '*poésie*' of steak and kidney *pudding*, not pie, with mashed potatoes and a big scoop of boiled cabbage. *English* mustard, if you have it.

HILDA: (Menacing whisper) Rumpole! Behave yourself!

WAITER: This . . . 'pudding' . . . is not on our menu.

RUMPOLE: 'Your pleasure is our delight.' It says that on your menu. Couldn't you ask Cookie if she could delight me? Along those lines.

WAITER: 'Cookie'? I do not know who *M'sieur* means by Cookie. Our *maître de cuisine* is Jean-Pierre O'Higgins himself. He is in the kitchen now.

RUMPOLE: How very convenient. Have a word in his shell-like, why don't you?

What keeps the Rumpole books going is that he is an ideal commentator on the changing scene and the increasingly eccentric behaviour of governments who seem determined to tell us how to live our lives. Rumpole takes the view that the business of government is to see that the trains run on time and the law courts are working efficiently. It should have nothing to do with telling us how to take a short rest after lunch or advising us how to cross the road or suggesting we eat up our green vegetables.

Even more seriously, he is appalled by the government using the existence of a few terrorists to justify abandoning all our ancient constitutional liberties.

My first client was a husband longing for a divorce but unable to persuade anyone to commit adultery with his wife. He was reduced to the terrifying expedient of putting on a false moustache and a pair of dark glasses and creeping publicly into his own mobile home, pretending to be his own co-respondent. Regrettably, when this was discovered, he was sent to prison for 'perverting the course of justice'.

It was occasions such as this which led my father to quote A. E. Housman's poem about the strange business of making laws.

'The laws of God, the laws of man'

The laws of God, the laws of man,
He may keep that will and can;
Not I: let God and man decree
Laws for themselves and not for me;
And if my ways are not as theirs
Let them mind their own affairs.
Their deeds I judge and much condemn,
Yet when did I make laws for them?
Please yourselves, say I, and they
Need only look the other way.
But no, they will not; they must still
Wrest their neighbour to their will,
And make me dance as they desire
With jail and gallows and hell-fire.
And how am I to face the odds

Of man's bedevilment and God's?
I, a stranger and afraid
In a world I never made.
They will be master, right or wrong;
Though both are foolish, both are strong.
And since, my soul, we cannot fly
To Saturn nor to Mercury,
Keep we must, if keep we can,
These foreign laws of God and man.

In spite of that exciting beginning, many of my cases at the Old Bailey turned out to be almost unbearably boring. None of such cases is included here, but I did end one month's tedium by saying, in my final speech, 'Members of the jury, you are to be congratulated on sitting through what must have been one of the most boring cases ever heard at the Old Bailey.' By way of revenge, the judge started his summing up by saying, 'Members of the jury, it may come as a surprise to you to know that it is not the sole purpose of the criminal law of England to entertain Mr Mortimer.'

I'm sure he was right about that, but boredom can be used as a formidable weapon in an argument (whereas it's death in a novel or the theatre of course). You can go on and on arguing endlessly to a judge who is continually looking at the clock and terrified of missing his train back to Haywards Heath. There's a decent chance that he will agree with you out of desperation.

More interesting than legal anecdotes are the letters, diaries and evidence of the accused. For instance, in the Thompson–Bywaters case. Edith Thompson was an incurable romantic, a sort of Madame Bovary of Kensington Gardens, though, of course, she lived in Ilford. She fell in love with a young seaman, Frederick Bywaters, and, it was said, induced him to stab her husband to death. This is how Edith Thompson wrote to Freddy Bywaters:

> On Thursday I went to the Waldorf for tea and while waiting in the vestibule by myself a gentleman came up, raised his hat and said, 'Are you Romance?' It seems he had an appointment with a lady he's corresponded with through the personal column . . .
>
> I am so stiff and sore today I can hardly move . . . This time last year you were able to rub me gradually and take that stiffness away. Do you remember?
>
> It was rather fun on Thursday at the garden party. They had swings and roundabouts and

flipflaps, coconut shies, Aunt Sallies, hoopla and all that sort of thing. I went in for them all and shocked a lot of people, I think. I don't care though. I'd got a rather posh frock on, white georgette with rows of jade ribbon and my white fur and a large hat, but all that didn't deter me from going into a fried-fish shop in Snaresbrook and buying fish and chips. Getting it home was the worst part – it absolutely smelt the bus out. I didn't mind – it was rather fun – only I wished you had been with me.

I think two halves would have enjoyed themselves better than one half by herself.

Goodbye for now, darlingest pal to Peidi.

Edith Thompson and her lover were both hanged in 1923. The Court of Appeal said it was rather an ordinary sort of case.

As I continued in my legal career I decided to become a QC (Queer Customers is what Rumpole calls them). To become a QC you need to go through a strange initiation ceremony. You have to go down to the House of Lords and swear an oath to help the Queen whenever she is in trouble. She has been in plenty of trouble but hasn't sent for me yet.

To swear this oath you have to wear a strange uniform, black patent-leather shoes, black silk stockings, black knee breeches with diamond buttons, a tail coat, a long silk gown and a wig with sort of spaniels' ears so you can't hear what's going on.

I was standing in Fleet Street waiting for the car to take me down to the House of Lords, wearing this uniform, when an old judge came hobbling by. 'Mortimer!' he cried. 'How are you keeping your silk stockings up?'

'More or less by faith, hope and prayer,' I told him.

'I'll give you a tip,' said the judge. 'There's a wonderful shop in Baker Street which sells suspender belts designed for the outsize hospital matron.'

And so he left me, and I've always felt that it must come as a great relief to the criminals of England to know that when they are being sent down for ten years the judge is, in all probability, wearing a suspender belt designed for an outsize hospital matron.

As a QC I began to do more important cases and I started to talk to juries. I have every respect for juries. I think they take their duties very seriously and have come back with decisions which I may not have liked but which have always been justifiable on the evidence. Sometimes they go to sleep in court, but everyone goes to sleep in court from time to time.

There was one notable case in which the prosecutor was taking a woman complainant through her evidence. He asked her to repeat what the man in the dock had said to her and she refused to do so, saying it would be too embarrassing. The sympathetic judge said he quite understood and instructed that she should be given a piece of paper and a pencil and write the dreaded words down. What she wrote down was 'Would you care for a screw?' The judge directed that that should be folded and handed to the jury.

So it was taken across the court. Number one jury person read it with interest, handed it on to number two, and so on. Number twelve jury person was an elderly gentleman who was fast asleep. Sitting next to him was a fairly personable young lady. She read the note with interest and woke up her sleeping neighbour and handed it to him. He read it with obvious surprise and delight, folded it up and put it in his wallet.

'Let that be handed up to me,' said the judge.

'I'm afraid not, My Lord,' the delighted recipient of the note said. 'It's a purely private matter.'

I defended a good many people who, it was suggested, might have been murderers. I found to my surprise that murderers are very agreeable clients. People in divorce cases are loathsome clients – they ring you up at two in the morning to say, 'You'll never guess what he's done now. Run off with the toast rack,' or, 'He's asking for custody of the bloody dog.'

Murderers find it harder to get to the telephone and all mine seemed extremely grateful for anything I was able to do for them. In many cases they had killed the one person in the world who was really bugging them and a sort of peace had come over their souls.

I know murder gets a very bad press, but I think that it is one of those crimes in which ordinary decent citizens can find themselves suddenly involved. I am not going to persuade you of this by my oratory, but I call as evidence this quotation from an Edinburgh newspaper:

While they were waiting at a bus stop in Clerimston, Mr and Mrs Daniel Thirsty were threatened by a Mr Robert Clear. 'He demanded that I give him my wife's purse,' said Mr Thirsty. Telling him that the purse was in her basket, 'I bent down, put my hands up her skirt, detached her artificial leg and hit him over the head with it . . . It was not my intention to do any more than frighten him off, but unhappily for us, he died.'

The other thing about murderers is that some of them weren't very good at it. If they had been better at it I would probably never have met them, but you must feel some pity for this totally unsuccessful murderer, whose bumbling attempts are chronicled in a local paper:

THE LEAST SUCCESSFUL ATTEMPT
TO MURDER A SPOUSE

Dwarfing all known records for matrimonial homicide, Mr Peter Scott of Southsea made seven attempts to kill his wife without her once noticing anything wrong. In 1960 he took out an insurance policy on his good lady which would bring him £250,000 in the event of her accidental death. Soon afterwards he placed a lethal dose of mercury in her strawberry flan, but it rolled out. Not wishing to waste this deadly substance, he next stuffed her mackerel with the entire contents of the bottle. This time she ate it, but with no side effects whatsoever.

Warming to the task, he then took his better half on holiday to Norway. Recommending the panoramic views, he invited her to sit on the edge of a cliff. She declined to do so, prompted by what she later describes as 'some sixth sense'. The same occurred only weeks later, when he urged her to savour the view from Beachy Head.

While his spouse was in bed with chickenpox, he started a fire outside her bedroom door, but some interfering busybody put it out. Undeterred, he started another fire and burnt down the entire flat at Taswell Road, Southsea. The wife of his bosom escaped uninjured.

Another time he asked her to stand in the middle of the road so that he could drive towards her and check if the brakes were working.

At no time did Mrs Scott feel that the magic had gone out of their marriage. Since it appeared nothing short of a small nuclear bomb would have alerted this good woman to her husband's intentions, he eventually gave up and confessed everything to the police. After the case a detective said that Mrs Scott had been 'absolutely shattered' when told of her husband's plot to kill her. She 'had not twigged it at all and was dumbstruck'.

Of course, defending in a murder case is a very serious business. You shouldn't ask too many questions and you shouldn't drink too much at lunchtime. I always drank at lunchtime, but never too much. One of my barrister friends drank a great deal too much one lunchtime, before he was due to go back and make a final speech in a murder case. He rose unsteadily to his feet and made what I think was one of the most realistic and well-phrased final speeches ever heard at the Old Bailey.

'Members of the jury,' he started somewhat uncertainly, but soon got into his stride, 'this is the moment at which I am meant to make a reasoned and moving speech on behalf of the accused. That will be followed by a fair and unbiased summing up from the learned judge and you will then retire and come to a just verdict. BUT,' he added, as terrible warning, 'the truth of the matter is that I am far too drunk to make a reasoned and moving speech, the learned judge has never been known to do a fair and unbiased summing up in his entire life and you all look far too stupid to come to a just verdict.' He sat down and they ordered a retrial.

To be accused of any crime must be a terrible thing and for no one more terrible than Oscar Wilde, when he was arrested at the Cadogan Hotel. This is how John Betjeman described it:

The Arrest of Oscar Wilde
at the Cadogan Hotel

He sipped at a weak hock and seltzer
As he gazed at the London skies
Through the Nottingham lace of the curtains
Or was it his bees-winged eyes?

To the right and before him Pont Street
Did tower in her new built red,
As hard as the morning gaslight
That shone on his unmade bed,

'I want some more hock in my seltzer,
And Robbie, please give me your hand –
Is this the end or beginning?
How can I understand?

'So you've brought me the latest *Yellow Book*:
And Buchan has got in it now:
Approval of what is approved of
Is as false as a well-kept vow.

'More hock, Robbie – where is the seltzer?
Dear boy, pull again at the bell!
They are all little better than *cretins*
Though this *is* the Cadogan Hotel.

'One astrakhan coat is at Willis's –
Another one's at the Savoy:
Do fetch my morocco portmanteau,
And bring them on later, dear boy.'

A thump, and a murmur of voices –
('Oh why must they make such a din?')
As the door of the bedroom swung open
And TWO PLAIN CLOTHES POLICEMEN
 came in:

'Mr. Woilde, we 'ave come for tew take yew
Where felons and criminals dwell:
We must ask yew tew leave with us quoietly
For this *is* the Cadogan Hotel.'

He rose, and he put down *The Yellow Book*.
He staggered – and, terrible-eyed,
He brushed past the palms on the staircase
And was helped to a hansom outside.

My father's blindness, terrible for him, gave me the
good fortune of having to read much of his favourite
poetry aloud. He introduced me to Robert Browning,
a poet who, I think, is undervalued nowadays.

This is a poem by Browning he liked very much.
It has the rhythm of a toccata, played by Galuppi
in the great days of Venice, the days of masques and
masquerades and great beauties born to die.

A Toccata of Galuppi's

I

Oh Galuppi, Baldassaro, this is very sad to find!
I can hardly misconceive you; it would prove me
    deaf and blind;
But although I take your meaning, 'tis with such a
    heavy mind!

II

Here you come with your old music, and here's all
    the good it brings.

What, they lived once thus at Venice where the
  merchants were the kings,
Where Saint Mark's is, where the Doges used to
  wed the sea with rings?

I I I

Ay, because the sea's the street there; and 'tis arched
  by . . . what you call
. . . Shylock's bridge with houses on it, where they
  kept the carnival:
I was never out of England – it's as if I saw it all.

I V

Did the young people take their pleasure when the
  sea was warm in May?
Balls and masks begun at midnight, burning ever to
  mid-day,
When they made up fresh adventures for the
  morrow, do you say?

V

Was a lady such a lady, cheeks so round and lips so
  red, –
On her neck the small face buoyant, like a bell-
  flower on its bed,

O'er the breast's superb abundance where a man
  might base his head?

VI

Well, (and it was graceful of them) – they'd break
  talk off and afford
– She, to bite her mask's black velvet – he, to
  finger on his sword,
While you sat and played Toccatas, stately at the
  clavichord?

VII

What? Those lesser thirds so plaintive, sixths diminished, sigh on sigh,
Told them something? Those suspensions, those
  solutions – 'Must we die?'
Those commiserating sevenths – 'Life might last!
  we can but try!'

VIII

'Were you happy?' – 'Yes.' – 'And are you still as
  happy?' – 'Yes. And you?'
– 'Then, more kisses!' – 'Did *I* stop them, when a
  million seemed so few?'
Hark, the dominant's persistence till it must be
  answered to!

IX

So, an octave struck the answer. Oh, they praised
    you, I dare say!
'Brave Galuppi! that was music! good alike at grave
    and gay!
I can always leave off talking when I hear a master
    play!'

X

Then they left you for their pleasure: till in due
    time, one by one,
Some with lives that came to nothing, some with
    deeds as well undone,
Death stepped tacitly and took them where they
    never see the sun.

XI

But when I sit down to reason, think to take my
    stand nor swerve,
While I triumph o'er a secret wrung from nature's
    close reserve,
In you come with your cold music till I creep
    thro' every nerve.

XII

Yes, you, like a ghostly cricket, creaking where a
    house was burned:
'Dust and ashes, dead and done with, Venice spent
    what Venice earned.
'The soul, doubtless, is immortal – where a soul
    can be discerned.

XIII

'Yours for instance: you know physics, something
    of geology,
'Mathematics are your pastime; souls shall rise in
    their degree;
'Butterflies may dread extinction, – you'll not die,
    it cannot be!

XIV

'As for Venice and her people, merely born to
    bloom and drop,
'Here on earth they bore their fruitage, mirth and
    folly were the crop:
'What of soul was left, I wonder, when the kissing
    had to stop?

XV

'Dust and ashes!' So you creak it, and I want the
  heart to scold.
Dear dead women, with such hair, too – what's
  become of all the gold
Used to hang and brush their bosoms? I feel chilly
  and grown old.

Browning was a great poet of character and the underlying sadness of human beings who can no longer understand each other comes alive in this poem.

My Last Duchess

That's my last Duchess painted on the wall,
Looking as if she were alive. I call
That piece a wonder, now: Fra Pandolf's hands
Worked busily a day, and there she stands.
Will't please you sit and look at her? I said
'Fra Pandolf' by design, for never read
Strangers like you that pictured countenance,
The depth and passion of its earnest glance,
But to myself they turned (since none puts by
The curtain I have drawn for you, but I)
And seemed as they would ask me, if they durst,
How such a glance came there; so, not the first
Are you to turn and ask thus. Sir, 'twas not
Her husband's presence only, called that spot
Of joy into the Duchess' cheek: perhaps

Fra Pandolf chanced to say 'Her mantle laps
Over my lady's wrist too much,' or 'Paint
Must never hope to reproduce the faint
Half-flush that dies along her throat': such stuff
Was courtesy, she thought, and cause enough
For calling up that spot of joy. She had
A heart – how shall I say? – too soon made glad,
Too easily impressed; she liked whate'er
She looked on, and her looks went everywhere.
Sir, 'twas all one! My favour at her breast,
The dropping of the daylight in the West,
The bough of cherries some officious fool
Broke in the orchard for her, the white mule
She rode with round the terrace – all and each
Would draw from her alike the approving speech,
Or blush, at least. She thanked men, – good! but
   thanked
Somehow – I know not how – as if she ranked
My gift of a nine-hundred-years-old name
With anybody's gift. Who'd stoop to blame
This sort of trifling? Even had you skill
In speech – (which I have not) – to make your
   will
Quite clear to such an one, and say, 'Just this
Or that in you disgusts me; here you miss,

Or there exceed the mark' – and if she let
Herself be lessoned so, nor plainly set
Her wits to yours, forsooth, and made excuse,
– E'en then would be some stooping; and I choose
Never to stoop. Oh sir, she smiled, no doubt,
Whene'er I passed her; but who passed without
Much the same smile? This grew; I gave
   commands;
Then all smiles stopped together. There she stands
As if alive. Will't please you rise? We'll meet
The company below, then. I repeat,
The Count your master's known munificence
Is ample warrant that no just pretence
Of mine for dowry will be disallowed;
Though his fair daughter's self, as I avowed
At starting, is my object. Nay, we'll go
Together down, sir. Notice Neptune, though,
Taming a sea-horse, thought a rarity,
Which Claus of Innsbruck cast in bronze for me!

There is a lot of talk now about sex education – who should give it, when it should be given, what should it contain. I didn't get much sex education at school, but when I was leaving my preparatory school and going on to a public school (which was in fact a private school) the headmaster gave us a talk which was designed to tell us all of the truth about life, love and the universe. I invented one such talk to put in my play *A Voyage Round My Father.*

HEADMASTER: You are the leavers! In a month or two you will go on to Great Public Schools, away from this warm cosy little establishment.

Ah now . . . Before I forget, Mrs Noah and I will be pleased to see you all for tea on Sunday. A trifling matter of anchovy paste sandwiches.

All come with clean fingernails, no boy to put butter on his hair. We had that trouble with the native regiments. They licked down their hair with butter. It went rancid in the hot weather. Unpleasant odour on parade. There's no law against a drop of water on the comb. Now . . . What was I going to tell you?

Ah! I was warning you about dreams. You'll have them. Oh, certainly you'll have them. And in the morning you may feel like saying to yourselves, 'You rotter! To have a dream like that!' Well, you can't help it. That's all. You simply can't help them. Not dreams. If you're awake of course, you can do something about it. You can change into a pair of shorts and go for a run across country. Or you can get into a bath and turn on the cold tap. You can quite easily do that. Your housemaster will understand. He'll understand if you should've been up to a French lesson, or Matins or some such thing. Simply say, 'Sir, I had to have a bath,' or a run, or whatever it is. Just say to Mr Raffles, or Humphrey Stiggler, or Percy Parr, just say, Mr Parr, or Mr Raffles, dependent on which school you're at of course, this is what I felt the need to do. He'll understand perfectly. Another thing! Simply this. When sleeping, always lie on the right side. Not on the face, for obvious reasons. Not on the back. Brings on dreams. Not on the left side. Stops the heart. Just on the right side . . . all the time.

Now then, to the most serious problems you're likely to run up against . . . Friends.

You may find that some boy from another class, or a house even, comes up to you and says, 'Let's be friends,' or even offers you a slice of cake. That's a very simple one, a perfectly simple one to deal with. Just say loudly, 'I'm going straight to tell the Housemaster.' Straight away. No hesitation about it. Remember, the only real drawback to our Great Public School system is unsolicited cake – Have you got that very clear? Go straight and tell the Housemaster.

That was my sex education. My friends' sisters seemed to find that their first experience of love was with their ponies. John Betjeman wrote about such a character.

Hunter Trials

It's awf'lly bad luck on Diana,
Her ponies have swallowed their bits;
She fished down their throats with a spanner
And frightened them all into fits.

So now she's attempting to borrow.
Do lend her some bits, Mummy, *do*;
I'll lend her my own for to-morrow,
But to-day I'll be wanting them too.

Just look at Prunella on Guzzle,
The wizardest pony on earth;
Why doesn't she slacken his muzzle
And tighten the breech on his girth?

I say, Mummy, there's Mrs. Geyser
And doesn't she look pretty sick?
I bet it's because Mona Lisa
Was hit on the hock with a brick.

Miss Blewitt says Monica threw it,
But Monica says it was Joan,
And Joan's very thick with Miss Blewitt,
So Monica's sulking alone.

And Margaret failed in her paces,
Her withers got tied in a noose,
So her coronets caught in the traces
And now all her fetlocks are loose.

Oh, it's me now. I'm terribly nervous.
I wonder if Smudges will shy.
She's practically certain to swerve as
Her Pelham is over one eye.

★　★　★

Oh, wasn't it naughty of Smudges?
Oh, Mummy, I'm sick with disgust.
She threw me in front of the Judges
And my silly old collarbone's bust!

As I have said, I have always loved, even adored, Lord Byron. His Lordship's mixture of common sense and romanticism, of conservatism and revolutionary fervour, of Puritanism and sensuality are all exactly to my taste. Here he is, observing an execution with true, lucid indifference and writing about it to his publisher John Murray:

The day before I left Rome I saw three robbers guillotined. The ceremony – including the 'masqued' priests; the half-naked executioners; the bandaged criminals; the black Christ and his banner; the scaffold and the soldiery; the slow procession, and the quick rattle and heavy fall of the axe; the splash of the blood, and the ghastliness of the exposed heads – is altogether more impressive than the vulgar and ungentlemanly dirty 'new drop', and dog-like agony of infliction upon the sufferers of the English sentence. Two of these men behaved calmly enough, but the first of the three died with great terror and reluctance, which was very horrible. He would not lie down; then his neck was too large for the aperture, and the priest was obliged to drown his exclamations by still louder exhortations. The head was off before the eye could trace the blow; but from an attempt to draw back the head, notwithstanding it was held forward by the hair, the first head was cut off close to the ears; the other two were taken off more cleanly. It is better than the oriental way, and (I should think) than the axe of our ancestors. The pain seems little; and yet the effect to the spectator, and the preparation to the criminal, are very striking and chilling.

The first turned me quite hot and thirsty, and made me shake so that I could hardly hold the opera glass (I was close, but determined to see, as one should see every thing, once, with attention); the second and third (which shows how dreadfully soon things grow indifferent), I am ashamed to say, had no effect on me as a horror, though I would have saved them if I could.

It is some time since I heard from you – the 12th April I believe.

Yours Ever Truly

B

'My hand shook so that I could hardly hold the opera glass' – the perpetual attitude of the writer in the face of experience.

Act Two

The second half of the performance starts with e e
cummings bringing us back from the hard reality of
writing to the wonderful fantasy of life and love.

mr youse needn't be so spry

mr youse needn't be so spry
concernin questions arty
each has his tastes but as for i
i likes a certain party
gimme the he-mans solid bliss
for youse ideas i'll match youse
a pretty girl who naked is
is worth a million statues

From this we speculate on the strange situation of so many beautiful and wonderful girls who have married the most appalling husbands. Robert Graves has views on the subject.

A Slice of Wedding Cake

Why have such scores of lovely, gifted girls
    Married impossible men?
Simple self-sacrifice may be ruled out,
    And missionary endeavour, nine times out
        of ten.

Repeat 'impossible men': not merely rustic,
    Foul-tempered or depraved
(Dramatic foils chosen to show the world
    How well women behave, and always have
        behaved).

Impossible men: idle, illiterate,
    Self-pitying, dirty, sly,

For whose appearance even in city parks
    Excuses must be made to casual passers-by.

Has God's supply of tolerable husbands
    Fallen, in fact, so low?
Or do I always over-value woman
  At the expense of man?
                Do I?
                    It might be so.

And now we have poems on the joys, terrors and embarrassments of love, starting with a piece from the *Greek Anthology*.

Seduced Girl

With wine and words of love and every vow
He lulled me into bed and closed my eyes,
A sleepy, stupid innocent . . . so now I dedicate the
    spoils of my surprise
The silk that bound my breasts, my virgin zone,
Goodness, remember we were all alone
And he was strong – and I was half asleep.

And this poem by Eleanor Brown deals with the awkward situation of an ex-boyfriend who wants the writer to become tremendously good friends with his new girlfriend. As you can imagine, the poem is called 'Bitcherel'.

Bitcherel

You ask what I think of your new acquisition;
and since we are now to be 'friends',
I'll strive to the full to cement my position
with honesty. Dear – it depends.

It depends upon taste, which must not be
    disputed;
for which of us *does* understand
why some like furnishings pallid, and muted,
their cookery wholesome and bland?

There isn't a *law* that a face should have features,
it's just that they generally *do*;

God couldn't give colour to all of his creatures,
and only gave wit to a few.

I'm sure she has qualities, much underrated,
that compensate amply for this,
along with a charm that is so understated
it's easy for people to miss.

And if there are some who choose clothing to
    flatter
what beauties they think they possess,
when what's underneath has no shape, does it
    matter
if there is no shape to the dress?

It's not that I think she is *boring*, precisely,
That isn't the word I would choose;
I know there are men who like girls who talk
    nicely
And always wear sensible shoes.

It's not that I think she is vapid and silly;
it's not that her voice makes me wince;
but – chilli con carne without any chilli
Is only a plateful of mince . . .

Here's another variation on the theme from Kingsley
Amis.

Nothing to Fear

All fixed: early arrival at the flat
Lent by a friend, whose note says *Lucky sod*;
Drinks on the tray; the cover-story pat
And quite uncheckable; her husband off
Somewhere with all the kids till six o'clock
(Which ought to be quite long enough);
And all worth while: face really beautiful,
Good legs and hips, and as for breasts – my God.
What about guilt, compunction and such stuff?
I've had my fill of all that cock;
It'll wear off, as usual.

Yes, all fixed. Then why this slight trembling,
Dry mouth, quick pulse-rate, sweaty hands,
As though she were the first? No, not impatience,
Nor fear of failure, thank you, Jack.

Beauty, they tell me, is a dangerous thing,
Whose touch will burn, but I'm asbestos, see?
All worth while – it's a dead coincidence
That sitting here, a bag of glands
Tuned up to concert pitch, I seem to sense
A different style of caller at my back,
As cold as ice, but just as set on me.

Love spans the centuries and can even bridge the generation gap, as lucky old Lord Rochester's young lady said.

A Song of a Young Lady to Her Ancient Lover

1.

Ancient person, for whom I
All the fluttering youths defy,
Long be it ere thou grow old,
Aching, shaking, crazy, cold,
But still continue as thou art,
Ancient person of my heart.

2.

On thy withered lips and dry
Which like barren furrows lie,
Brooding kisses I will pour,
Shall thy youthful heat restore.
Such kind show'rs in autumn fall

And a second spring recall:
Nor from thee will ever part,
Ancient person of my heart.

3.

Thy nobler part, which but to name
In our sex would be counted shame,
By age's frozen grasp possess'd
From his ice shall be releas'd,
And, soothed by my reviving hand,
In former warmth and vigour stand.
All a lover's wish can reach,
For thy joy my love shall teach,
And for thy pleasure shall improve
All that art can add to love.
Yet still I love thee without art,
Ancient person of my heart.

And here is John Betjeman touchingly describing the sad situation of certain lonely women.

Business Girls

From the geyser ventilators
   Autumn winds are blowing down
On a thousand business women
   Having baths in Camden Town.

Waste pipes chuckle into runnels,
   Steam's escaping here and there,
Morning trains through Camden cutting
   Shake the Crescent and the Square.

Early nip of changeful autumn,
   Dahlias glimpsed through garden doors,
At the back precarious bathrooms
   Jutting out from upper floors;

And behind their frail partitions
   Business women lie and soak,
Seeing through the draughty skylight
   Flying clouds and railway smoke.

Rest you there, poor unbelov'd ones,
   Lap your loneliness in heat.
All too soon the tiny breakfast,
   Trolley-bus and windy street!

The miscellany becomes more cheerful with an unin-
hibited invitation written by Allen Ginsberg.

Fie My Fum

Pull my daisy,
Tip my cup,
Cut my thoughts
For coconuts,

Bone my shadow,
Dove my soul,
Set a halo
On my skull,

Ark my darkness,
Rack my lacks,
Bleak my lurking,
Lark my looks,

Start my Arden,
Gate my shades,
Silk my garden,
Rose my days,

Whore my door,
Stone my dream,
Milk my mind
And make me cream,

Say my oops,
Ope my shell,
Roll my bones,
Ring my bell,

Pope my parts,
Pop my pot,
Poke my pap,
Pit my plum.

That's an invitation to true love probably just as true as Auden's more complete and elaborate love poem in the form of a lullaby.

Lay Your Sleeping Head

Lay your sleeping head, my love,
Human on my faithless arm;
Time and fevers burn away
Individual beauty from
Thoughtful children, and the grave
Proves the child ephemeral:
But in my arms till break of day
Let the living creature lie,
Mortal, guilty, but to me
The entirely beautiful.

Soul and body have no bounds:
To lovers as they lie upon
Her tolerant enchanted slope
In their ordinary swoon,

Grave the vision Venus sends
Of supernatural sympathy,
Universal love and hope;
While an abstract insight wakes
Among the glaciers and the rocks
The hermit's carnal ecstasy.

Certainty, fidelity
On the stroke of midnight pass
Like vibrations of a bell,
And fashionable madmen raise
Their pedantic boring cry:
Every farthing of the cost,
All the dreaded cards foretell,
Shall be paid, but from this night
Not a whisper, not a thought,
Not a kiss nor look be lost.

Beauty, midnight, vision dies:
Let the winds of dawn that blow
Softly round your dreaming head
Such a day of sweetness show
Eye and knocking heart may bless,
Find the mortal world enough;
Noons of dryness see you fed

By the involuntary powers,
Nights of insult let you pass
Watched by every human love.

I feel a little guilty about my treatment of judges. Many of them have asked me why all the judges in the Rumpole stories are either malignant or twits. I've tried to explain that the Greek theory of drama requires a quarrel between Rumpole and the judge, and I try to rectify the situation by telling a story about a sympathetic judge. I find him sympathetic because he tells this story which is against himself. I'll call him Reg Dean, because that's not his name. In the days when he was a barrister, he tells us, he defended Bessie, the local brothel-keeper, and got her off. She gave him a big kiss afterwards in the presence of the newspapers and promised to give him an extremely valuable reward.

I should make it clear that Reg's wife, Noreen, was one of those severe unsmiling women with a one-piece bosom who seem to spend a great deal of their lives ironing. The special reward Bessie the local brothel-keeper was offering was a free visit to any of the girls in her house.

Reg returned home full of pride and excitement at having won a difficult case. Noreen responded by continuing to iron silently. Finally Reg was driven to tell her, 'Bessie was so pleased with me that she wanted to give me a present and the present she offered was, any time I felt like it, I could go down to her house and have one free. On the house.'

There was a prolonged silence and then Noreen stood up her iron and, having considered the matter, pronounced her verdict:

'I know what I think you should do, Reg. You finish up your tea, and then you go down to Bessie's house and disappoint some other woman.'

Love, as you all know, is an extremely dangerous business. Most dangerous of all if you are around Maida Vale, which is where I used to live in London, and happen to catch the eye of William Plomer's 'French Lisette'.

> Who strolls so late, for mugs a bait
> In the mists of Maida Vale,
> Sauntering past a stucco gate
> Fallen, but hardly frail?
>
> You can safely bet that it's French Lisette,
> The pearl of Portsdown Square,
> On the game she has made her name
> And rather more than her share.
>
> In a coat of cony with her passport phoney
> She left her native haunts,
> For an English surname exchanging *her* name
> And took up with a ponce.

Now a meaning look conceals the hook
Some innocent fish will swallow,
Chirping 'Hullo, Darling' like a cheeky starling
She'll turn and he will follow,

For her eyes are blue and her eyelids too
And her smile's by no means cryptic,
Her perm's as firm as if waved with glue,
She plies an orange lipstick.
And orange-red is her perky head
Under a hat like tiny pie –

A pie on a tart, it might be said,
Is redundant, but oh, how spry!
From distant tundra to snuggle under her
Chin a white fox conveyed,
And winks and leerings and Woolworth earrings
She's all set up for trade.

Now who comes here replete with beer?
A quinquagenarian clerk
Who in search of life has left 'the wife'
And 'the kiddies' in Tufnell Park.

Dear Sir, beware! For sex is a snare
And all is not true that allures.
Good Sir. Come off it! She means to profit
By this little weakness of yours.

Ah, if only he knew that concealed from view
Behind a 'fold-weave' curtain
Is her fancy man, called Dublin Dan,
His manner would be less certain.

His bedroom eyes would express surprise,
His attitude less languor,
He would watch his money, not call her 'Honey'
And be seized with fear or anger.

Of the old technique one need scarcely speak,
But oh, in the quest for Romance
'Tis folly abounding in a strange surrounding
To be divorced from one's pants.

A happy sex life is no doubt important in marriage. A friend of mine noticed that, when having sex on films or television, women at the moment of climax utter alluring little moaning noises which seemed to him to add greatly to the joy of the occasion. He asked his wife if she would moan at the vital moment and she said, 'Of course, dear, that would be no trouble at all.' As their lovemaking built to its climax he said, 'Now, darling, moan.' But her only answer was, 'I had to go down to Tesco's three times this morning . . .'

Sex may be dangerous after a certain age. When a family's grandmother was asked why grandpa died, she said, 'We had sex regularly every Sunday morning in time to the sound of the church bell, but if that bloody Italian ice-cream van hadn't driven up, Grandpa would be alive today.'

'Marriage,' an American friend once observed, 'is like the hurricanes we have here in Florida. It starts off with all that sucking and blowing and you end up by losing your house.'

Reasonable men and women have to make their compromises in marriage. Here are Mirabell and Mrs Millamant in William Congreve's *The Way of the World*, when she is setting out her stipulations for a working married relationship.

MRS MILLAMANT: My dear liberty, shall I leave thee? My faithful solitude, my darling contemplation, must I bid you then adieu? Ay, adieu. My morning thoughts, agreeable wakings, indolent slumbers, all ye *douceurs*, ye *sommeils du matin*, adieu. I can't do't, 'tis more than impossible – positively, Mirabell, I'll lie a-bed in a morning as long as I please.

MIRABELL: Then I'll get up in the morning as early as I please.

MRS MILLAMANT: Ah! Idle creature, get up when you will. And, d'ye hear, I won't be called names after I'm married; positively I won't be called names.

MIRABELL: Names?

MRS MILLAMANT: Ay, as wife, spouse, my dear,

joy, jewel, love, sweet-heart, and the rest of that nauseous cant, in which men and their wives are so fulsomely familiar – I shall never bear that. Good Mirabell, don't let us be familiar or fond, nor kiss before folks, like my Lady Fadler and Sir Francis . . . Let us never visit together, nor go to a play together, but let us be very strange and well-bred. Let us be as strange as if we had been married a great while, and as well-bred as if we were not married at all.

MIRABELL: Have you any more conditions to offer? Hitherto your demands are pretty reasonable.

MRS MILLAMANT: Trifles . . . to have no obligation upon me to converse with wits that I don't like, because they are your acquaintances, or to be intimate with fools, because they may be your relations. Come to dinner when I please, dine in my dressing-room when I'm out of humour, without giving a reason. To have my closet inviolate; to be sole empress of my tea-table, which you must never presume to approach without first asking leave. And lastly, wherever I am, you shall always knock

at the door before you come in. These arti-
cles subscribed, if I continue to endure you
a little longer, I may by degrees dwindle into
a wife.

We'll go no more a-roving

So, we'll go no more a-roving
　　So late into the night,
Though the heart be still as loving,
　　And the moon be still as bright.

For the sword outwears its sheath,
　　And the soul wears out the breast,
And the heart must pause to breathe,
　　And love itself have rest.

Though the night was made for loving,
　　And the day returns too soon,
Yet we'll go no more a-roving
　　By the light of the moon.

That was Byron at his most lyrical.

Love, writing, the law. I am conscious that these extracts have not dealt with the world of politics. When I was a schoolboy I formed a one-man Communist cell at Harrow. The war was on and when Germany and Russia were allies I was urged from the King Street headquarters to organize a go-slow on my factory floor. Well, my factory floor was the Classical Fourth, and the go-slow didn't take a lot of organizing.

Later, when Hitler attacked Russia, I was urged to go down to the factory floor and speed up production, so I tried to get everyone to read Virgil twice as fast. Finally I grew impatient with politicians, who seemed to me to spare far too little thought for life, love and the pursuit of happiness. Take, for instance, this quotation from the *Peking Worker's Daily*:

Love between man and woman consumes energy and wastes time . . . on the other hand, love of the Party and of the Chairman, Mao-Tse-Tung, takes no time at all and is in itself a powerful tonic.

Today I suppose I would describe myself as a middle-of-the-road liberal anarchist. However, I have grown impatient with party politics, which always have to create imaginary enemies, the Reds, or the Tories, or the unions, in order to keep a totally spurious feeling of excitement on the political scene. Our dependence on a political enemy is wonderfully expressed in C. P. Cavafy's poem.

Waiting for the Barbarians

What are we waiting for, all gathered in the forum?

  The barbarians are coming today.

Why is there such inertia in the Senate?
Why are the senators just sitting there, not passing laws?

  Because the barbarians are coming today.

What laws should the senators pass now?
When the barbarians come they'll draft our
    laws.

Why is the emperor out of bed so early?
Why is he sitting at the city's main gate,
crowned and looking so formal on his throne?

> Because the barbarians are coming today
> and the emperor is arranging a welcome
> for their leader. In fact, he has prepared
> a formal decree, and on the parchment
> he has written numerous titles and marks of
>   respect.

Why have our two consuls and praetors come out
    today,
dressed in their embroidered red togas?
Why are they wearing bracelets set with amethysts,
and rings with bright, shining emeralds?
Why are they carrying their official staffs
inlaid with silver and gold?

> Because the barbarians are coming today,
> and such things are known to dazzle barbarians.

Why don't the famous orators arrive as they always
  do
to pontificate at length and expound on their
  views?

    Because the barbarians are coming today,
    and they are bored by eloquence and long
       discourse.

Why has this anxiety come upon us all at once,
why such confusion? (How serious all the faces!)
Why are the streets and squares emptying so
  quickly,
and all the people returning to their homes so
  subdued?

    Because night came and the barbarians never
      appeared.
    Later some of our men arrived from the
      borders
    and gave us the news: there were no more
      barbarians.

What are we going to do now, without barbarians?
Those people, they were a kind of solution.

So if the barbarians are something we have to invent to keep up our enthusiasm for largely illusory political differences, what of the true basis of existence – what of religious belief? I was born, I must admit, without a religious sense and when I was young I didn't greatly miss it.

My father was a Darwinian evolutionist – who told me that a horse could not be created by anyone in seven centuries, let alone seven days. At school, church services always seemed to be conducted by partially shell-shocked padres with vivid memories of strafing Jerry in the First World War, and a great enthusiasm for bombing him again in the next. Yet I am fascinated by clerics and never miss the opportunity of a good argument with a bishop. However, I cannot stomach the idea of eternal life, which my father described as living for ever and ever in a great transcendental hotel with nothing to do in the evenings. Nor can I forgive an omnipotent creator who damns the results of his omnipotence.

There is, however, a religious point of view I can understand, the feeling that I have now occasionally when I'm alone in my garden in the country, or awake at night with the wind whipping through the beech wood or down the long, empty valley outside my window, lit up by a storm.

'no time ago'

no time ago
or else a life
walking in the dark
i met christ

jesus (my heart
flopped over
and lay still
while he passed) as

close as I'm to you
yes closer
made of nothing
except loneliness

That was e e cummings again.

I've talked a lot about my father, and the house he built in the country where I now live with my wife and children, where all my other children come. He really taught me nothing, particularly he never told me the difference between right and wrong, and yet when I read, or when I write, it's his standards I remember, for he taught me everything.

Up to the end he delighted in using and misusing quotations from Shakespeare. There is a terrible scene in *King John*, a play not often performed, in which Hubert the Gaoler is about to put out little Prince Arthur's eyes. Hubert's line to the executioners is: 'When I strike my foot upon the bosom of the ground, rush forth, and bind the boy.' My father used to say, 'Rush forth and bind the boy? Sounds like the name of a rather undesirable firm of solicitors.' Whenever he saw a solicitor he hadn't met before, he used to say, 'Are you from Rushforth and Bindtheboy by any chance?'

When You are Old

When you are old and gray and full of sleep,
  And nodding by the fire, take down this book,
  And slowly read, and dream of the soft look
Your eyes had once, and of their shadows deep;

How many loved your moments of glad grace,
  And loved your beauty with false love or true;
  But one man loved the pilgrim soul in you,
And loved the sorrows of your changing face;

And bending down beside the glowing bars,
  Murmur, a little sadly, how love fled
  And paced upon the mountains overhead,
And hid his face amid a crowd of stars.

That was Yeats facing old age.

Writing in 'The Tower', Yeats had a clear view of the most important things in the life of a poet.

> I have prepared my peace
> With learned Italian things
> And the proud stones of Greece,
> Poet's imaginings
> And memories of love,
> Memories of the words of women,
> All those things whereof
> Man makes a superhuman
> Mirror-resembling dream.

I have chosen this Thomas Hardy as an epitaph for him, or for me, or for all of us who spend our best days in the country and notice the things that matter.

Afterwards

When the Present has latched its postern beneath
　　my tremulous stay,
　And the May month flaps its glad green leaves
　　like wings,
Delicate-filmed as new-spun silk, will the neigh-
　bours say,
　'He was a man who used to notice such things'?

If it be in the dusk when, like an eyelid's soundless
　　blink,
　The dewfall-hawk comes crossing the shades to
　　alight
Upon the wind-warped upland thorn, a gazer may
　　think,
　'To him this must have been a familiar sight.'

If I pass during some nocturnal blackness, mothy
and warm,
   When the hedgehog travels furtively over the
   lawn,
One may say, 'He strove that such innocent creatures should come to no harm,
   But he could do little for them; and now he is
   gone.'

If, when hearing that I have been stilled at last,
they stand at the door,
   Watching the full-starred heavens that winter sees,
Will this thought rise on those who will meet my
face no more,
   'He was one who had an eye for such mysteries'?

And will any say when my bell of quittance is
heard in the gloom,
   And a crossing breeze cuts a pause in its outroll-
   ings,
Till they rise again, as they were a new bell's
boom,
   'He hears it not now, but used to notice such
   things'?

And finally, a poem by Winthrop Praed.

Good-Night to the Season

Good-night to the Season! 'tis over!
Gay dwellings no longer are gay;
The courtier, the gambler, the lover,
Are scattered like swallows away:
There's nobody left to invite one,
Except my good uncle and spouse;
My mistress is bathing at Brighton,
My patron is sailing at Cowes:
For want of a better employment,
Till Ponto and Don can get out,
I'll cultivate rural enjoyment,
And angle immensely for trout.

Good-night to the Season! – the lobbies,
Their changes, and rumours of change,
Which startled the rustic Sir Bobbies,
And made all the Bishops look strange:

The breaches, and battles, and blunders,
Performed by the Commons and Peers;
The Marquis's eloquent thunders,
The Baronet's eloquent ears:
Denouncings of Papists and treasons,
Of foreign dominion and oats;
Misrepresentations of reasons,
And misunderstandings of notes.

Good-night to the Season! – the buildings
Enough to make Inigo sick;
The paintings, and plasterings, and gildings
Of stucco, and marble, and brick;
The orders deliciously blended,
From love of effect, into one;
The club-houses only intended,
The palaces only begun;
The hell where the fiend, in his glory,
Sits staring at putty and stones,
And scrambles from story to story,
To rattle at midnight his bones.

Good-night to the Season! The dances,
The fillings of hot little rooms,
The glancings of rapturous glances

The fancyings of fancy costumes;
The pleasures which Fashion make duties,
The praisings of fiddles and flutes,
The luxury of looking at beauties,
The tedium of talking to mutes;
The female diplomatists, planners
Of matches for Laura and Jane,
The ice of her Ladyship's manners,
The ice of his Lordship's champagne.

Good-night to the Season! The rages
Led off by the chiefs of the throng,
The Lady Matilda's new pages,
The Lady Eliza's new song;
Miss Fennel's macaw, which at Boodle's
Is held to have something to say;
Mrs Splendic's musical poodles,
Which bark 'Batti Batti' all day;
The pony Sir Araby sported,
As hot and as black as a coal,
And the Lion his mother imported,
In bearskins and grease, from the Pole.

Good-night to the Season! The Toso,
So very majestic and tall;

Miss Ayton, whose singing was so-so,
And Pasta, divinest of all;
The labour in vain of the Ballet,
So sadly deficient in stars;
The foreigners thronging the Alley,
Exhaling the breath of cigars;
The 'loge' where some heiress, how killing,
Environed with Exquisites sits,
The lovely one out of her drilling,
The silly ones out of their wits.

Good-night to the Season! The splendour
That beamed in the Spanish Bazaar;
Where I purchased – my heart was so tender –
A card-case, – a pasteboard guitar, –
A bottle of perfume, – a girdle, –
A lithographed Reigo full-grown,
Whom Bigotry drew on a hurdle
That artists might draw him on stone, –
A small panorama of Seville, –
A trap for demolishing flies, –
A caricature of the Devil, –
And a look from Miss Sheridan's eyes.

Good-night to the Season! The flowers
Of the grand horticultural fete,
When boudoirs were quitted for bowers,
And the fashion was not to be late;
When all who had money and leisure
Grew rural o'er ices and wines,
All pleasantly toiling for pleasure,
All hungrily pining for pines,
And making of beautiful speeches,
And marring of beautiful shows,
And feeding on delicate peaches,
And treading on delicate toes.

Good-night to the Season! Another
Will come with its trifles and toys,
And hurry away like its brother,
In sunshine, and odour, and noise.
Will it come with a rose or a briar?
Will it come with a blessing or curse?
Will its bonnets be lower or higher?
Will its morals be better or worse?
Will it find me grown thinner or fatter,
Or fonder of wrong or of right,
Or married, – or buried? – no matter,
Good-night to the Season, Good-night!

Cast List

Emily Best
Richard Briers
Clive Conway
Christine Croshaw
Sinéad Cusack
Joanna David
Gabrielle Drake
Marsha Fitzalan-Howard
Jill Freud
Gerald García
Lisa Goddard
Celia Imrie
Geraldine James
Simon James
Louise Jameson
Phyllida Law
Jon Lord
Nichola McAuliffe

Philip Mountford
Angharad Rees
Llinos Richards
Anton Rodgers

Permissions

Kingsley Amis's 'Nothing to Fear' (© Kingsley Amis 1967) is reprinted by kind permission of Jonathan Clowes Ltd., London, on behalf of Kingsley Amis. W. H. Auden's 'As I Walked Out One Evening' and 'Lullaby', from *Collected Poems*, are reprinted with permission from Faber and Faber Ltd. John Betjeman's 'The Arrest of Oscar Wilde at the Cadogan Hotel', 'Hunter Trials' and 'Business Girls' from *Collected Poems* (© 2006) are reprinted with permission from Aitken Alexander Ltd. Eleanor Brown's 'Bitcherel' is reprinted with permission from Bloodaxe Books. C. P. Cavafy's 'Waiting for the Barbarians', from *Selected Poems*, is reprinted with permission from Penguin Books Ltd. E. E. Cummings' 'Mr, youse needn't be' and 'No Time Ago', from *Selected Poems*, is reprinted with permission from Faber and Faber Ltd. Lines from Allen Ginsberg's 'Fie My Fum', from *Collected Poems* 1947–1997 (© 2006) are reprinted by kind permission of the Wylie Agency on behalf of the Allen Ginsberg Trust. 'A Slice of Wedding Cake' by Robert Graves is reprinted with permission from Carcanet Press Ltd. 'French Lisette: A Ballad of Maida Vale' by William Plomer, from *Collected Poems*, is reprinted with permission from The Random House Group Ltd. Lines from W. B. Yeats' 'The Tower' and 'When You Are Old' are reprinted with permission from A. P. Watt Ltd on behalf of Gráinne Yeats.